CONTENTS

The Slow Climb	1
The Slow Climb	2
Introduction	4
Chapter 1	7
Chapter 2	12
Chapter 3	19
Chapter 4	24
Chapter 5	31
Chapter 6	38
Chapter 7	44
Chapter 8	51
Chapter 9	59
Chapter 10	66
30-Day Personal Growth, Faith, and Weight-Loss Challenge	73
Call to Action	97
About The Author	101

THE SLOW CLIMB

The Path to an Extraordinary Life.

Winsome Campbell

THE SLOW CLIMB

The Path to an Extraordinary Life

Written by Winsome Campbell

Copyright © [2024] Winsome Campbell
All rights reserved.

No part of this publication may be reproduced, distributed, or transmitted in any form or by any means, including photocopying, recording, or other electronic or mechanical methods, without the prior written permission of the publisher, except in the case of brief quotations embodied in critical reviews and certain other noncommercial uses permitted by copyright law.

For permissions, please contact:

Winsome Campbell
Website: www.winsomecampbell.com

ISBN: 9798336929089
Palm Beach, Florida
Cover design by [Winsome Campbell]
Interior design by [Winsome Campbell]

Disclaimer: The information contained in this book is for general information purposes only. The author and publisher make no representations or warranties of any kind about the completeness, accuracy, or reliability of the information contained in this book. Any reliance you place on such information is therefore strictly at your own risk.

Printed in [United States of America]

First Edition
2024

INTRODUCTION

Dear Readers,

In this book "The Slow Climb: The Path to an Extraordinary Life, I share my personal story of transformation. I explain how the slow, deliberate climb in life is often the most sustainable path to achieving extraordinary results. By embracing patience, persistence, and faith, readers can unlock the potential that lies within them. What readers can expect from the book is me emphasizing the focus on personal growth, faith, and wellness.

Every extraordinary journey starts with a single, often hesitant step. Before we can soar, we must first crawl, learn, and grow through the experiences that shape us. My own journey was not one of instant transformation, nor was it free from setbacks and challenges. Instead, it was a slow climb—a deliberate and intentional pursuit of a life that felt not just fulfilling, but extraordinary. I'm Winsome Campbell, and I'm here to guide you through this process of slow, sustainable growth that leads to lasting change.

In a world that glorifies speed and instant gratification, we often feel pressured to reach our goals as quickly as possible. The allure of quick fixes and overnight success stories can make us feel inadequate if we're not progressing at breakneck speed. But the truth is, lasting transformation rarely happens overnight. Just as a mountain climber must scale the terrain with caution and care, we, too, must take our time on the climb toward a truly extraordinary life.

For me, this journey started when I realized that chasing immediate results often led to burnout and disappointment. I wanted something deeper—something that would endure beyond the fleeting moments of success. That's when I began to understand the value of the slow climb. By embracing patience, persistence, and faith, I discovered that true transformation happens not in a sprint but in the steady, intentional steps we take each day.

In this book, I'll share the lessons I've learned along the way and offer a roadmap for your own journey. Whether you're seeking personal growth, a deeper connection to your faith, or a healthier lifestyle, the principles of the slow climb can help you achieve your goals in a meaningful and lasting way. Together, we'll explore how to cultivate habits that stick, how to nurture your body and soul, and how to transform your setbacks into stepping stones toward success.

This is not just a book about quick wins; it's about embracing the process of growth, no matter how long it takes. It's about trusting that each small step, each moment of perseverance, brings you closer to the extraordinary life you've always dreamed of. As you read through these chapters, you'll find practical tools, faith-based inspiration, and the encouragement you need to stay committed to your path.

By the end of this journey, you'll realize that the slow climb was never about reaching the summit as fast as possible. Instead, it's about learning to enjoy the process, to grow in faith and resilience, and to become the best version of yourself along the way. I invite you to embrace this journey with an open heart and mind, knowing that every step forward, no matter how small, brings you closer to the extraordinary life that awaits.

So, let's begin this journey together. The climb may be slow, but the destination is worth every step. Welcome to The Slow Climb: The Path to an Extra-Ordinary Life.

CHAPTER 1

The Power of Starting Small

Starting with small steps in any journey, whether it's personal growth, weight loss, or building faith is the key for achieving the remarkable. In this chapter I provide real-life examples and encourages readers to celebrate small victories, laying the foundation for long-term success.

Every great achievement begins with the smallest of steps. It's easy to look at the extraordinary lives of others and wonder how they got there, but rarely do we see the beginning of their journey. We don't see the tiny, almost insignificant actions that ultimately led to something remarkable. I want to show you the immense power of starting small and how these humble beginnings can lead to extraordinary results in your life.

We live in a culture that glorifies big leaps and overnight success, but real transformation doesn't happen in an instant. It happens in the daily decisions, the small, consistent efforts that build momentum over time. Whether you're embarking on a journey of personal growth, striving to lose weight, or strengthening your faith, the key is to start with small, manageable steps.

When I first began my weight-loss journey, I was overwhelmed by the magnitude of the changes I wanted to make. I had big dreams, but those dreams felt so far out of reach that I didn't know where to begin.

It was daunting to think about transforming my lifestyle, changing my eating habits, and incorporating regular exercise into my daily routine. I envisioned a better version of myself, full of energy and confidence, but the path to get there seemed incredibly long and winding.

What I learned, though, was that the key to unlocking extraordinary change was to start with the smallest, most achievable actions. Instead of focusing on the entire mountain looming ahead, I chose to concentrate on one step at a time. I began by setting a simple yet significant goal: a daily 10-minute walk. This wasn't about becoming a marathon runner overnight or overhauling my entire diet in one fell swoop—it was about creating a habit that I could maintain and build upon.

As I embarked on this first step, I noticed that it wasn't just the physical act of walking that made a difference; it was the mental shift that accompanied it. Each evening, after dinner, I laced up my sneakers and stepped outside, savoring the fresh air and the feeling of accomplishment that washed over me. Those first few walks were invigorating, and they became a daily ritual that I looked forward to.

Once I had settled into this routine, I began to layer on additional small changes. I started paying closer attention to my food choices, focusing on incorporating more fruits and vegetables into my meals instead of trying to eliminate all my favorite foods. I experimented with healthier recipes and discovered new ingredients that I genuinely enjoyed. I took joy in the process rather than viewing it as a punishment for past indulgences.

As the weeks passed, something remarkable happened. I began to feel stronger, both physically and mentally. The small victories—finishing my daily walk without stopping, choosing a healthy meal option when dining out, and feeling more energetic throughout the day—built upon one another, reinforcing my commitment to this journey. Each step I took felt like a victory lap, and I could see how these small actions were paving the way for larger transformations.

I also discovered the importance of celebrating my

achievements, no matter how small they seemed. Acknowledging my progress kept me motivated and focused. I started to create a journal to document my journey, writing down not just my weight loss but how I felt after completing a workout or how proud I was for making a healthy dinner. This practice became a valuable tool, allowing me to reflect on how far I had come and encouraging me to keep moving forward.

With every small change, my confidence grew. I found myself exploring new physical activities I had previously dismissed. What began with that 10-minute daily walk eventually evolved into trying out dance classes, walking for 30-minutes 3-4 times per week, and even getting a personal trainer to help me stay accountable. I realized that weight loss was about more than just the numbers on a scale; it was about nurturing a healthier relationship with my body and discovering joys I hadn't anticipated.

Looking back now, I can see that the journey was less about reaching an endpoint and more about the cumulative effects of countless small decisions. Each step I had taken not only brought me closer to my weight-loss goals but also transformed my mindset toward health and wellness. I came to understand that extraordinary change doesn't occur overnight; it's a gradual process built on consistency, patience, and a willingness to embrace every little step along the way.

In the end, what started as a seemingly insurmountable challenge became a rewarding adventure. I learned to trust the process, savor the little achievements, and embrace the journey itself. Each small action led to significant results, allowing me to create a healthier, happier lifestyle that felt much more sustainable. And now, as I continue on this path, I carry with me the invaluable lesson that even the greatest transformations begin with a single, courageous step forward.

CHAPTER 2

Building a Solid Foundation

In this chapter, I will teach you how to create a strong foundation for success by developing daily habits. I share strategies for incorporating faith-based practices, such as prayer and meditation, into your daily routines while also focusing on healthy living.

A house built on shaky ground will inevitably crumble, no matter how magnificent it appears on the outside. The same is true for our lives—if we want to build something extraordinary, we must first ensure that the foundation is solid and unshakable. The daily habits you will be creating will serve to nurture both the mind and body, as well as the soul.

Success, in any area of life, doesn't happen by accident. It's the result of consistent effort and intentionality. The habits we cultivate every day, no matter how small they may seem, have the power to shape our future. But in order to build habits that last, we must anchor them in something deeper than fleeting motivation. We need a foundation that will keep us steady, even when life gets challenging.

For me, that foundation has always been rooted in faith. My relationship with God has provided me with the strength, guidance, and resilience to face life's challenges. Incorporating faith-based practices into my daily routine has been essential to my growth and transformation. Whether through prayer, meditation, or simply taking a moment to reflect on the blessings in my life, these practices have grounded me and given me the clarity I need to stay focused on my goals.

I'll share with you how to develop your own daily routines that nurture your spiritual, mental, and physical well-being. We'll explore simple yet powerful practices that can help you build a solid foundation for your journey, no matter where you are starting from.

The Power of Daily Prayer and Meditation

Starting your day with prayer or meditation can set the

tone for everything that follows. It's a way to connect with your inner self and with God, aligning your intentions with your values. Even if you're new to these practices, starting small—just a few minutes each morning—can make a significant impact over time. This practice creates a sense of peace and centeredness that you can carry with you throughout the day, no matter what challenges arise.

Developing Consistent Habits

Building a solid foundation isn't just about grand gestures; it's about the consistent, daily actions that accumulate over time. Small habits, done repeatedly, can lead to massive change. Whether it's committing to a few minutes of exercise each day, drinking more water, or spending time in gratitude, these habits compound and strengthen your foundation.

I'll guide you through the process of choosing habits that align with your goals and values and help you stay accountable to them. I took the time to acquire a Habit Tracker to help me stay focus on what is most important in my journey. Whether it was drinking water regularly, working out or achieving your savings goals, the habit tracker will certainly get you there.

Nourishing Your Body and Mind

Just as we need to nourish our spirits, we must also take care of our bodies and minds. In this chapter, we'll explore how to create a balanced lifestyle that supports both your health and your personal growth. This includes paying attention to your diet, staying active, and practicing self-care. A strong foundation of physical health naturally enhances our mental and emotional well-being, creating a harmonious balance that empowers us to flourish in all areas of life.

When we talk about a balanced lifestyle, nutrition is a crucial component. The food we consume not only sustains our energy levels but also influences our mood, cognitive function, and overall health. Eating a varied diet rich in whole foods, including fruits, vegetables, whole grains, lean proteins, and healthy fats, provides our bodies with essential nutrients that promote optimal functioning.

It's important to cultivate a mindful approach to eating. This means not only being aware of what we eat but also why we eat. Are we reaching for snacks out of genuine hunger, or are we using food to cope with stress, boredom, or emotional turbulence? Developing awareness can help us create healthier eating habits, making strategic choices that nourish us physically and emotionally.

Meal planning can be an effective tool in this regard. By preparing meals ahead of time, we can avoid the pitfalls of convenience foods that tend to be high in sugars, unhealthy fats, and empty calories. Additionally, setting aside time each week to plan meals not only ensures we eat better but also reduces stress during busy weekdays.

Staying Active

Physical activity is another cornerstone of a balanced lifestyle. Regular exercise is vital for maintaining a healthy body, but its benefits extend far beyond physical fitness. Exercise has been shown to improve mental health by reducing symptoms of anxiety and depression, enhancing mood, and boosting self-esteem. It's also an excellent way to release pent-up energy and stress, providing a mental reset that allows us to face challenges with greater resilience.

Finding an activity that you enjoy is key to staying active. Whether it's dancing, swimming, hiking, yoga, or joining a local sports team, engaging in physical activity should feel more like a pleasurable part of your day rather than a chore. Aim for a blend of cardiovascular exercises, strength training, and flexibility practices to ensure a well-rounded approach to fitness.

Incorporating movement into your daily routine doesn't have to be daunting. Simple changes, such as taking the stairs instead of the elevator, walking or biking to nearby destinations, or scheduling a daily walk during lunch breaks, can contribute significantly to your overall activity level. The key is consistency; establishing a routine can help make physical activity a habitual part of your life.

Practicing Self-Care

Self-care is an essential practice that encompasses various activities and habits that prioritize our mental and emotional well-being. In our fast-paced world, it's easy to neglect self-care, often leading to burnout and fatigue.

However, prioritizing time for activities that refresh and recharge us is critical for sustaining personal growth and health.

Self-care can take many forms, from indulging in a relaxing bath, practicing meditation, journaling, spending time in nature, or simply setting aside time to read a book. It's about deliberately carving out moments in our day to unwind and check in with ourselves. Regular self-reflection allows us to identify our needs—be it emotional support, creative expression, or social connections—and make adjustments accordingly.

Building Inner Resilience

A balanced lifestyle isn't merely about maintaining physical health; it's also about building resilience. Challenges and stress are inevitable, but how we respond to them can be transformative. Developing tools to manage stress effectively—such as mindfulness practices, problem-solving skills, and a supportive social network—can significantly enhance our capacity to navigate life's ups and downs.

Engaging in practices such as mindfulness meditation can help us cultivate a sense of presence and awareness, allowing us to observe our thoughts and emotions without judgment. This practice can reduce stress, increase our capacity for empathy toward ourselves and others, and foster a deeper connection to our inner selves.

Cultivating Community Connections

Finally, part of a balanced life involves fostering connections with others. Building a supportive community is vital for our well-being, as relationships provide us with love, encouragement, and resources during tough times. Engaging with friends, family, or groups that share your interests can offer a sense of belonging and foster personal growth.

Volunteering can also be a rewarding way to connect with others and make a difference in the community. By sharing your time and talents, you not only contribute to a greater cause but also enrich your own life, gaining perspective and satisfaction from helping others.

To wrap up this chapter, embracing a balanced lifestyle involves a holistic approach that nurtures our bodies and minds while supporting our personal growth. By paying attention to our diet, staying active, practicing self-care, and cultivating meaningful relationships, we create a solid foundation for health and well-being. Remember, the journey to balance is unique for everyone, and it's essential to be patient and compassionate with ourselves as we navigate this path. Small, consistent efforts yield significant results; each step we take towards a healthier lifestyle ultimately leads to a richer, more fulfilling life.

CHAPTER 3

Facing the Mountains of Fear and Doubt

Addressing the challenges of fear and self-doubt that often arise when embarking on a new journey is critical to for an extraordinary journey. I provide practical advice for overcoming these mental barriers and I also discus how faith can help conquer fear and build confidence.

Embarking on a new journey is often accompanied by fear and self-doubt. These formidable obstacles can feel like towering mountains, casting shadows over our aspirations and making the climb seem almost impossible. It's not uncommon to experience a rush of anxiety when starting something new—whether it's a personal growth initiative, a weight-loss goal, or a spiritual quest. But understanding how to confront and overcome these mental barriers is crucial for moving forward and achieving lasting success.

Fear and self-doubt are natural responses to stepping out of our comfort zones. They are our mind's way of protecting us from potential failure or disappointment. However, if left unchecked, these feelings can paralyze us and prevent us from taking the necessary steps toward our goals. The key is to recognize these feelings for what they are —temporary and surmountable obstacles—and to equip ourselves with strategies to overcome them.

1. Acknowledging and Understanding Your Fear

The first step in overcoming fear and self-doubt is to acknowledge and understand them. Instead of ignoring or suppressing these emotions, it's important to confront them head-on. Ask yourself: What exactly am I afraid of? What are my doubts telling me? By identifying the root causes of your fear, you can begin to address them more effectively.

For instance, if you're afraid of starting a new fitness routine, ask yourself what specifically worries you. Is it the fear of not seeing results? Are you concerned about judgment from others? By pinpointing the specific fears, you can address them with targeted strategies.

Understanding that these fears are common and part of the process can also provide some comfort and perspective.

2. Reframing Your Mindset

Once you've identified your fears, the next step is to reframe your mindset. Self-doubt often stems from a negative inner dialogue that tells us we're not good enough or that we'll fail. To counter this, you need to consciously shift your thoughts toward positivity and possibility.

One effective technique is to replace negative self-talk with positive affirmations. For example, if you find yourself thinking, "I'll never be able to achieve this goal," counter it with, "I am capable of making progress, one step at a time." Reframing your mindset involves recognizing these negative thoughts and deliberately choosing to replace them with affirmations that support your success.

3. Taking Small, Courageous Steps

The journey of overcoming fear is often about taking small, courageous steps, rather than making giant leaps. These small steps might seem insignificant on their own, but they accumulate over time and build confidence. Each time you face a fear and take action despite it, you strengthen your resilience and build a foundation of confidence.

Start with manageable goals that push you slightly out of your comfort zone. If you're fearful of public speaking, begin by practicing in front of a mirror or with a trusted friend. Gradually increase the size of your audience as you become more comfortable. Each small success will help dispel your fear and build your confidence.

4. Harnessing the Power of Faith

Faith can be a powerful ally in overcoming fear and self-doubt. Believing in a higher purpose or in your ability to achieve your goals provides a source of strength and encouragement. Faith helps shift the focus from our limitations to the possibilities that lie ahead.

In times of fear, turning to prayer or spiritual practices can offer comfort and guidance. Reflect on scriptures or inspirational messages that resonate with you. For example, the verse "For God gave us a spirit not of fear but of power and love and self-control" (2 Timothy 1:7) can be a powerful reminder of your inherent strength and potential.

Faith also involves trusting the process and believing that each step you take is part of a larger plan. Even when progress feels slow or obstacles arise, faith can help you maintain perspective and stay motivated. By surrendering your fears to a higher power and seeking guidance through prayer or meditation, you can find the courage to continue moving forward.

5. Building a Support System

Finally, building a strong support system can make a

significant difference in overcoming fear and self-doubt. Surround yourself with people who encourage and uplift you. Share your goals and challenges with trusted friends or mentors who can provide advice, offer support, and celebrate your successes with you.

Having a support system also means seeking professional help if needed. Sometimes, talking to a coach, therapist, or counselor can provide valuable insights and strategies for managing fear and building confidence. Don't hesitate to reach out for help if you find that fear and self-doubt are overwhelming your progress.

Therefore, facing the mountains of fear and doubt is an integral part of any transformative journey. By acknowledging your fears, reframing your mindset, taking small steps, harnessing the power of faith, and building a supportive network, you can overcome these barriers and move closer to your goals. Remember, fear is a natural part of growth, but it doesn't have to dictate your path. With perseverance and the right strategies, you can conquer these obstacles and continue climbing toward the extraordinary life you're destined to achieve.

CHAPTER 4

Facing the Mountains of Fear and Doubt

F aith is a core component of the slow climb to an extraordinary life. In this chapter I m going to guide you on how to deepen your faith and use it as a source of strength during difficult times. I outline scriptures, affirmations, and journaling exercises to help readers strengthen their spiritual foundation.

In the journey toward an extraordinary life, faith acts as the bedrock upon which everything else is built. It's the inner strength that propels us forward when we're faced with challenges, and it provides the guidance and assurance we need to stay the course. Strengthening your faith muscles is not merely about religious practice; it's about cultivating a profound trust and resilience that supports you through every stage of your climb.

1. Understanding the Role of Faith in Personal Growth

Faith is more than a belief system; it's a powerful force that can transform your entire approach to life. It's about trusting in something greater than yourself and finding meaning and purpose in every step of your journey. Faith helps you stay grounded, even when the path is uncertain or challenging. It's the inner conviction that, despite obstacles, you are moving in the right direction and that there is a purpose behind every experience.

In the context of personal growth, faith serves as a constant source of motivation and inspiration. It encourages you to persevere through difficulties and to view setbacks as opportunities for growth rather than failures. By strengthening your faith, you align your actions with your values and maintain a sense of direction, even when the climb gets steep.

2. Building a Daily Faith Practice

To strengthen your faith muscles, it's essential to establish a daily practice that nurtures your spiritual well-being. This practice doesn't have to be elaborate; consistency is more important than complexity. Here are some practical steps to incorporate faith into your daily routine:

Morning Devotions:

Begin your day with a moment of reflection or prayer. This can set a positive tone for the day and help you focus on your intentions. Choose a scripture or an affirmation that resonates with you and meditate on its meaning.

Daily Affirmations:

Create a list of positive affirmations rooted in your faith. Repeat these affirmations throughout the day to reinforce your beliefs and boost your confidence. For example, "I am guided and supported by a higher power in all that I do" can serve as a reminder of your inner strength and guidance.

Gratitude Journaling:

At the end of each day, take a few moments to write down what you're grateful for. This practice helps shift your focus from what's lacking to what's abundant in your life. It also cultivates a mindset of appreciation and positivity.

3. Embracing Scripture and Inspirational Readings

Scripture and inspirational readings can offer profound insights and encouragement. Incorporate these into your daily routine to deepen your understanding and connection with your faith. Here are some ways to integrate scripture into your life:

Daily Scripture Reading:
Set aside time each day to read a passage from your sacred texts. Reflect on its message and consider how it applies to your current situation. This practice can provide comfort and wisdom, helping you navigate challenges with faith.

Scripture Memorization:

Memorize key verses that resonate with you. Having these verses readily available in your mind can provide strength and guidance when you face difficulties. For instance, memorizing Philippians 4:13, "I can do all things through Christ who strengthens me," can be a powerful reminder of your resilience.

Inspirational Books and Devotionals:

Read books or devotionals that inspire and uplift you. Choose texts that align with your beliefs and offer practical advice for applying faith to everyday life. These readings can offer new perspectives and reinforce your spiritual practices.

4. Engaging in Spiritual Community

Being part of a spiritual community can significantly enhance your faith journey. Connecting with others who share your beliefs provides support, encouragement, and a sense of belonging. Here's how to engage with your spiritual community:

Join a Faith Group:

Participate in a faith-based group or study circle. This can be a church group, a Bible study class, or an online faith community. Sharing experiences and discussing spiritual topics with others can strengthen your understanding and commitment.

Seek Mentorship:

Find a mentor or spiritual advisor who can offer guidance and support. A mentor can provide valuable insights, help you navigate challenges, and offer encouragement as you deepen your faith.

Volunteer and Serve:

Engaging in acts of service and volunteering can strengthen your faith and connect you with like-minded individuals. Serving others is a way to express your beliefs in action and make a positive impact on your community.

5. Practicing Trust and Surrender

One of the most powerful aspects of faith is learning to trust and surrender. Trusting in the process means believing that even when things don't go according to plan, there is a greater purpose at work. Surrendering to this process involves letting go of the need to control every outcome and accepting that some things are beyond your control.

To practice trust and surrender:

Release Control:

Acknowledge the things you cannot control and focus on what you can influence. Trust that everything will unfold as it's meant to and that you are supported through every step of your journey.

Prayer and Reflection:

Use prayer or meditation to express your concerns and seek guidance. Trust that your prayers are heard and that you are being guided toward the right path.

Embrace Uncertainty:

Understand that uncertainty is a natural part of life. Embrace it as an opportunity for growth and trust that your faith will guide you through the unknown.

Finally, strengthening your faith muscles is a crucial part of the slow climb to an extraordinary life. By building a daily faith practice, embracing scripture, engaging with a spiritual community, and practicing trust and surrender, you can deepen your connection with your spiritual self and find the strength to overcome challenges. Faith is not just a belief but a source of power that can transform your life and support you in reaching your fullest potential. As you continue on your journey, let faith be your guide, your anchor, and your source of inspiration, propelling you toward the extraordinary life you're meant to live.

WINSOME CAMPBELL

CHAPTER 5

Nourishing Your Body and Soul

In this chapter, I focus on the connection between physical health and spiritual well-being. I offer tips on creating a balanced diet, staying active, and nourishing the soul through positive thinking and gratitude.

Achieving an extraordinary life requires more than just a strong mindset and unwavering faith. It demands a harmonious balance between physical health and spiritual well-being. Just as a well-nourished body can enhance your daily functioning and overall vitality, a nourished soul can uplift and sustain you through life's challenges.

1. Creating a Balanced Diet

The food we consume is fuel for our bodies and minds. A balanced diet not only supports physical health but also contributes to mental clarity and emotional stability. Here are some key principles for creating a nourishing diet:

Embrace Whole Foods:
Focus on incorporating whole, unprocessed foods into your diet. Fruits, vegetables, whole grains, lean proteins, and healthy fats provide essential nutrients that support overall health. Aim to fill half of your plate with vegetables and fruits, a quarter with lean protein, and the remaining quarter with whole grains.

Hydrate Adequately:

Staying hydrated is crucial for maintaining energy levels and supporting bodily functions. Drink plenty of water throughout the day and consider incorporating herbal teas or infused water for variety. Proper hydration also aids in digestion and helps keep your skin healthy and glowing.

Moderation and Balance:

While it's important to focus on nutritious foods, it's equally important to enjoy your meals and treat yourself occasionally. Strive for moderation rather than perfection. Allow yourself the occasional indulgence without guilt, and remember that balance is key to long-term success.

Mindful Eating:

Practice mindful eating by paying attention to your hunger cues and savoring each bite. Avoid distractions such as TV or smartphones during meals. Eating mindfully can help you enjoy your food more and prevent overeating.

2. Staying Active

Regular physical activity is essential for maintaining a healthy body and mind. Exercise not only improves physical fitness but also has a profound impact on mental and emotional well-being. Here's how to incorporate activity into your life:

Find Activities You Enjoy:

Choose physical activities that you find enjoyable and fulfilling. Whether it's walking, dancing, yoga, or swimming, engaging in activities you love makes it easier to stay committed. Find what resonates with you and make it a regular part of your routine.

Set Realistic Goals:

Start with achievable goals and gradually increase the intensity or duration of your workouts. Setting small, incremental goals can help you build confidence and maintain motivation. For example, aim to walk for 15 minutes a day and gradually extend the time as you become more comfortable.

Incorporate Movement into Your Day:

Look for opportunities to stay active throughout the day. Take the stairs instead of the elevator, go for a brisk walk during breaks, or incorporate short bursts of exercise into your routine. Small changes can add up and contribute to overall physical health.

Rest and Recovery:

Allow your body time to rest and recover between workouts. Adequate rest is crucial for muscle repair and overall well-being. Incorporate rest days into your routine and listen to your body's signals to avoid overtraining.

3. Nourishing the Soul Through Positive Thinking

Just as physical health supports your body, positive thinking nurtures your soul. Cultivating a positive mindset can enhance your emotional resilience and overall quality of life. Here's how to foster positive thinking:

Practice Affirmations:

Use positive affirmations to reinforce self-belief and optimism. Repeat statements such as, "I am capable of achieving my goals," or "I embrace each day with a positive outlook." Affirmations can help shift your mindset and build self-confidence.

Challenge Negative Thoughts:

Pay attention to negative self-talk and actively challenge it. When you notice yourself thinking negatively, ask yourself whether these thoughts are based on facts or assumptions. Replace negative thoughts with positive or neutral alternatives.

Surround Yourself with Positivity:

Surround yourself with positive influences, whether it's uplifting people, inspiring books, or motivating media. Engage in activities that bring you joy and fulfillment, and distance yourself from negativity.

4. Cultivating Gratitude

Gratitude is a powerful practice that can significantly enhance your sense of well-being and happiness. By focusing on what you're grateful for, you shift your perspective from what's lacking to what's abundant in your life. Here's how to cultivate gratitude:

Gratitude Journaling:

Keep a gratitude journal where you write down three things you're grateful for each day. This practice helps you focus on the positive aspects of your life and fosters a sense of appreciation.

Express Appreciation:

Make it a habit to express gratitude to those around you. Acknowledge and thank people for their kindness and support. Simple acts of appreciation can strengthen relationships and create a positive atmosphere.

Reflect on Blessings:

Take time to reflect on the blessings and achievements in your life. Consider the progress you've made, the support you've received, and the small joys that bring you happiness. Reflecting on these blessings can reinforce a sense of contentment and fulfillment.

5. Integrating Physical and Spiritual Wellness

The connection between physical health and spiritual well-being is profound. By integrating practices that nurture both aspects, you create a harmonious balance that supports your overall growth. For example, consider incorporating spiritual elements into your physical activities:

Mindful Movement:

Combine physical exercise with mindfulness practices. For instance, practice yoga with a focus on breathing and meditation, or take a mindful walk in nature, appreciating the beauty around you.

Prayerful Reflection:

Use exercise as a time for reflection or prayer. As you engage in physical activity, focus on gratitude and connection with your spiritual self. This integration of mind, body, and spirit can enhance the benefits of both practices.

Finally, nourishing your body and soul is essential for achieving an extraordinary life. By creating a balanced diet, staying active, fostering positive thinking, and cultivating gratitude, you lay the groundwork for a healthy and fulfilling journey. Remember that both physical and spiritual well-being are interconnected, and nurturing each aspect supports your overall growth. Embrace these practices as integral parts of your climb, and let them guide you toward a life of vitality, resilience, and joy.

CHAPTER 6

Embracing Patience in the Climb

Patience is a virtue, especially on the slow climb. Keep dialed in this this book and encourage yourself. When you embrace the process, even when progress seems slow, you are succeeding in the slow climb. I will also share personal anecdote and practical tips for cultivating patience and perseverance.

In a world that often prioritizes instant gratification,

patience can seem like a rare and challenging virtue. Yet, when embarking on the slow climb to an extraordinary life, patience is not just a virtue—it's a crucial ingredient for success. This chapter delves into the art of embracing patience, offering practical tips and personal anecdotes to help you navigate the journey with grace and persistence.

1. Understanding the Role of Patience in Personal Growth

Patience is more than just waiting; it's about maintaining a positive attitude and remaining steadfast in your goals, even when progress appears slow. It's the quiet strength that enables you to persevere through obstacles, setbacks, and periods of stagnation. Without patience, the climb toward your dreams can become frustrating and disheartening.

The slow climb is characterized by gradual progress, incremental achievements, and often, a considerable amount of time. This process can be challenging, especially when results are not immediately visible. However, patience allows you to stay focused on your long-term vision, trusting that every step, no matter how small, brings you closer to your goals.

2. Personal Anecdotes: Lessons in Patience

Throughout my own journey, I've learned firsthand the value of patience. There were times when I felt stuck or disheartened by the slow pace of my progress. For instance, when I was working toward my weight loss goals, the results were not as rapid as I had hoped. I remember weeks when the scale barely budged, and it was easy to feel discouraged.

However, it was during these times that I learned to embrace patience. I focused on the small victories, like improved energy levels and healthier habits, rather than just the numbers on the scale. By shifting my focus to the process rather than the outcome, I was able to stay motivated and continue making positive changes.

Another example is my experience with building my writing career. Initially, the path seemed daunting, and the progress was slow. There were moments of self-doubt and frustration, but I learned to value the journey itself. Each step, each revision, and each piece of feedback was part of a larger process that ultimately led to significant growth and success.

3. Cultivating Patience: Practical Tips

Cultivating patience requires intentional effort and practice. Here are some practical tips to help you embrace patience and navigate the slow climb with resilience:

Set Realistic Goals:

Break down your larger goals into smaller, manageable steps. Setting realistic, incremental goals can make the process feel more achievable and provide a sense of accomplishment along the way. Celebrate each small victory, as these moments build momentum and reinforce your patience.

Focus on the Journey, Not Just the Destination:

Shift your focus from the end result to the journey itself. Embrace the experiences, lessons, and growth that occur along the way. By valuing the process, you cultivate a sense of fulfillment and satisfaction that goes beyond immediate outcomes.

Practice Mindfulness:

Mindfulness techniques can help you stay present and appreciate the current moment. Engage in mindfulness practices such as meditation, deep breathing, or journaling to center yourself and reduce anxiety about future results. Mindfulness helps you stay grounded and patient as you navigate the climb.

Stay Positive and Persistent:

Maintain a positive outlook, even when progress seems slow. Remind yourself of the reasons you embarked on this journey and the benefits of perseverance. Positive self-talk and affirmations can boost your confidence and resilience, helping you stay committed to your goals.

Seek Support and Guidance:

Surround yourself with supportive individuals who encourage and motivate you. Share your goals and challenges with trusted friends, mentors, or coaches who can offer guidance and perspective. Having a support network can provide reassurance and remind you that you're not alone in your journey.

4. Embracing Setbacks as Opportunities

Setbacks are an inevitable part of the climb, but they can also serve as valuable opportunities for growth. When faced with obstacles or delays, view them as chances to learn and adapt. Reflect on what the setback can teach you and how you can use it to strengthen your resolve and refine your approach.

For instance, if you encounter a setback in your weight loss journey, consider what might have contributed to it. Use the experience to adjust your strategy, whether it's modifying your workout routine or reassessing your diet. Embrace setbacks as learning experiences that offer insights and resilience.

5. The Power of Perseverance

Perseverance is the driving force that keeps you moving forward, even when patience feels like a challenge. It's the determination to continue despite difficulties and setbacks. Cultivating perseverance involves staying committed to your goals, maintaining a positive attitude, and trusting that your efforts will eventually lead to success.

Remind yourself that every step, no matter how small, is

progress. Perseverance helps you push through obstacles and stay focused on your long-term vision. By combining patience with perseverance, you create a powerful synergy that propels you toward your extraordinary life.

In this chapter, I talked about embracing patience in the climb is essential for achieving lasting success and fulfillment. By understanding the role of patience, learning from personal experiences, and applying practical tips, you can navigate the journey with resilience and grace. Remember that the slow climb is not a hindrance but a crucial part of your growth and transformation. Trust the process, celebrate each small victory, and remain steadfast in your pursuit of an extraordinary life. With patience and perseverance, you will find that the climb becomes not just a path to success but a rewarding and enriching journey in itself.

CHAPTER 7

Transforming Setbacks into Stepping Stones

Every journey comes with setbacks. You are doing a great job. To transform setbacks into stepping stones, I will focus on how to turn challenges and obstacles into opportunities for growth. There is no magic wand you can wave to lose weight or achieve other burning goals. I will teach you how to reframe your mindset and view setbacks as stepping stones to success.

Setbacks are an inevitable part of any journey toward achieving greatness. They come in various forms—unexpected obstacles, failures, or delays—and can often feel discouraging. However, it's not the setbacks themselves that define our success, but rather how we respond to them. This chapter explores how to transform setbacks into stepping stones, turning challenges into opportunities for growth and progress.

1. Embracing the Reality of Setbacks

Setbacks are not signs of failure but rather integral parts of the growth process. Every successful person has faced obstacles and challenges along their journey. Understanding that setbacks are a natural and unavoidable aspect of pursuing goals can help you approach them with a more constructive mindset.

Recognize that setbacks provide valuable learning experiences. They can reveal areas for improvement, highlight weaknesses, and offer insights that may not be apparent during smooth sailing. By acknowledging setbacks as part of the process, you can shift your perspective and view them as opportunities for development rather than as insurmountable barriers.

2. Reframing Your Mindset

Reframing your mindset is crucial for transforming setbacks into stepping stones. Instead of viewing setbacks as failures, consider them as chances to learn and grow.

Here's how to reframe your thinking:

Change Your Perspective:

Look at setbacks from a different angle. Instead of focusing on what went wrong, ask yourself what you can learn from the experience. For example, if a project fails to meet expectations, analyze what aspects didn't work and how you can improve in the future.

Focus on the Positive: Identify any positive outcomes that may have resulted from the setback. Perhaps the challenge led you to discover new strategies, connect with supportive individuals, or gain a deeper understanding of yourself. Emphasizing these positive aspects can help you maintain motivation and resilience.

Set New Goals:

Use setbacks as a catalyst for setting new goals or adjusting your current ones. Reflect on what the setback has taught you and how you can incorporate those lessons into your revised goals. This proactive approach helps you stay focused and forward-looking.

3. Learning from Setbacks

Every setback offers valuable lessons. By examining the causes and consequences of the setback, you can gain insights that inform your future actions. Here's how to effectively learn from setbacks:

Conduct a Post-Mortem Analysis:

After experiencing a setback, take time to analyze what went wrong. Identify the factors that contributed to the setback and evaluate how you can address them. This analysis helps you understand the root causes and develop strategies to prevent similar issues in the future.

Seek Feedback:

Solicit feedback from others who may have insight into the situation. This can include mentors, colleagues, or friends who can provide constructive criticism and suggestions for improvement. External perspectives can offer valuable guidance and help you see the situation more objectively.

Reflect on Personal Growth:

Consider how the setback has contributed to your personal growth. Reflect on how you've developed resilience, problem-solving skills, or a greater understanding of your strengths and weaknesses. Recognizing your growth can reinforce your confidence and determination.

4. Developing Resilience Through Challenges

Resilience is the ability to bounce back from adversity and continue moving forward despite challenges. Developing resilience involves cultivating a mindset that embraces challenges and perseveres through difficulties. Here are some strategies to build resilience:

Cultivate a Growth Mindset:

Embrace the belief that challenges and setbacks are opportunities for growth. Adopting a growth mindset allows you to see obstacles as chances to develop new skills and strengthen your abilities.

Practice Self-Compassion:

Be kind to yourself during setbacks. Avoid self-criticism and negative self-talk. Instead, practice self-compassion by acknowledging your efforts and understanding that setbacks are a natural part of the journey.

Build a Support System:

Surround yourself with supportive individuals who can offer encouragement and advice during challenging times. Having a network of friends, family, or mentors can provide emotional support and practical guidance.

5. Turning Setbacks into Opportunities

Transforming setbacks into opportunities involves proactive steps to leverage the lessons learned and apply them constructively. Here's how to turn setbacks into stepping stones:

Innovate and Adapt:

Use setbacks as a chance to innovate and adapt. Consider alternative approaches or creative solutions that you may not have explored otherwise. Adaptability is key to overcoming challenges and finding new pathways to success.

Strengthen Your Determination:

Let setbacks fuel your determination and commitment to your goals. Use the experience as motivation to work harder and persist in the face of adversity. Reinforce your resolve by focusing on the larger purpose behind your goals.

Celebrate Resilience:

Acknowledge and celebrate your ability to overcome setbacks. Recognize the strength and resilience you've demonstrated and use it as a source of pride and motivation. Celebrating your progress helps build confidence and reinforces a positive mindset.

6. Real-Life Examples of Turning Setbacks into Success

Real-life examples of individuals who have transformed setbacks into success can serve as powerful sources of inspiration. Consider stories of famous personalities or everyday heroes who faced significant challenges but emerged stronger and more successful. Their experiences highlight the potential for growth and achievement that can arise from overcoming adversity.

For instance, J.K. Rowling faced numerous rejections before

finally publishing the Harry Potter series, which went on to become a global phenomenon. Her perseverance in the face of setbacks is a testament to the power of resilience and determination.

In this chapter, I discussed transforming setbacks into stepping stones is a vital aspect of achieving an extraordinary life. By embracing setbacks as learning opportunities, reframing your mindset, and developing resilience, you can navigate challenges with confidence and grace. Remember that setbacks are not the end of the road but rather a detour that can lead to new and unexpected opportunities. With each challenge you overcome, you build the strength and wisdom necessary to continue climbing toward your extraordinary goals.

CHAPTER 8

Elevating Your Relationships

Building extraordinary relationships is a key aspect of personal growth. Here I discus how to strengthen and elevate connections with loved ones, foster positive relationships, and remove toxic influences from one's life.

Building extraordinary relationships is essential to living a fulfilling and successful life. The connections we nurture with others can significantly impact our personal growth, happiness, and overall well-being.

1. Strengthening Connections with Loved Ones

Healthy, supportive relationships with family and friends are the cornerstone of personal growth and well-being. Strengthening these connections involves investing time and effort into meaningful interactions and showing appreciation for those who matter most.

Communicate Openly and Honestly:
Effective communication is the foundation of strong relationships. Make an effort to express your thoughts, feelings, and needs openly and honestly. Encourage others to do the same, creating a space where everyone feels heard and valued. Active listening—truly focusing on what the other person is saying without interrupting or judging—can deepen your connection and resolve misunderstandings.

Show Appreciation and Gratitude:

Regularly express your appreciation for the people in your life. Small gestures of gratitude, such as saying "thank you" or acknowledging someone's efforts, can go a long way in strengthening relationships. Make a habit of celebrating milestones, achievements, and everyday moments with those you care about.

Prioritize Quality Time:

In our busy lives, it's easy to let relationships take a

backseat. Make a conscious effort to spend quality time with loved ones. Plan activities that you all enjoy, whether it's a family dinner, a weekend outing, or simply spending time together at home. Quality time fosters deeper connections and creates lasting memories.

Support Each Other's Goals:

Show interest in and support for the goals and aspirations of those close to you. Encourage their endeavors and be a source of motivation and encouragement. By supporting each other's dreams, you strengthen the bond and contribute to each other's growth.

2. Fostering Positive Relationships

Positive relationships contribute to your overall happiness and personal development. Cultivating and maintaining these relationships involves surrounding yourself with people who uplift, inspire, and support you.

Build Trust and Respect:

Trust and respect are fundamental to positive relationships. Honor your commitments, be reliable, and show respect for others' boundaries and opinions. Trust takes time to build, but once established, it forms the basis of a strong and enduring relationship.

Surround Yourself with Uplifting Individuals:

Evaluate the people you interact with regularly and

consider their impact on your well-being. Surround yourself with individuals who inspire you, encourage your growth, and contribute positively to your life. Engage with people who share your values and goals, and who challenge and support you in a constructive manner.

Practice Empathy and Compassion:

Empathy involves understanding and sharing the feelings of others. Practice putting yourself in someone else's shoes and responding with compassion and kindness. Empathy strengthens relationships by fostering a sense of connection and mutual understanding.

Celebrate Others' Successes:

Be genuinely happy for the achievements and successes of those around you. Celebrate their victories as if they were your own and offer sincere congratulations and support. Sharing in the joy of others strengthens relationships and fosters a positive, collaborative environment.

3. Removing Toxic Influences

Toxic relationships can undermine your well-being and hinder your personal growth. Identifying and addressing toxic influences in your life is crucial for maintaining a healthy and positive environment.

Recognize the Signs of Toxicity:

Toxic relationships are characterized by patterns of

negativity, manipulation, and emotional harm. Signs include consistent criticism, lack of support, and behavior that leaves you feeling drained or unappreciated. Acknowledge these patterns and understand their impact on your well-being.

Set Boundaries:

Establish clear and healthy boundaries with individuals who exhibit toxic behavior. Communicate your needs and limits assertively, and be prepared to enforce them. Setting boundaries helps protect your emotional health and prevents others from overstepping their limits.

Limit Contact with Negative Influences:

If a relationship is consistently detrimental to your well-being, consider reducing or eliminating contact with the person. While this can be challenging, prioritizing your mental and emotional health is essential. Focus on building relationships that contribute positively to your life.

Seek Support if Needed:

If you find it difficult to navigate or address toxic relationships on your own, seek support from trusted friends, family members, or a professional counselor. Having an outside perspective can help you gain clarity and develop strategies for managing or removing toxic influences.

4. Nurturing New Connections

Building new, positive relationships can enrich your life and expand your support network. Here's how to nurture new connections and integrate them into your life:

Be Open to New Experiences:

Embrace opportunities to meet new people and explore new social settings. Attend events, join groups or clubs, or participate in community activities. Being open to new experiences increases the likelihood of forming meaningful connections.

Practice Authenticity:

Be yourself and allow others to see the real you. Authenticity attracts genuine connections and fosters trust. Share your interests, values, and passions openly, and seek out others who resonate with your true self.

Invest in Building Relationships:

Like any worthwhile endeavor, building new relationships requires time and effort. Invest in getting to know others, showing genuine interest, and nurturing the connection. Regular communication and shared experiences strengthen new relationships and pave the way for lasting bonds.

5. Enhancing Existing Relationships

Even in strong relationships, there is always room for

growth and enhancement. Here are ways to deepen existing connections and strengthen your bond:

Engage in Shared Activities:

Participate in activities or hobbies that you and the other person enjoy together. Shared experiences create opportunities for bonding and build a sense of camaraderie.

Address Conflicts Constructively:

Conflicts are a natural part of relationships, but how you handle them makes a difference. Address conflicts openly and constructively, focusing on resolution rather than blame. Practice active listening and seek mutual understanding to resolve disagreements amicably.

Continuously Invest in the Relationship:

Relationships require ongoing effort and attention. Regularly check in with the other person, express your appreciation, and make efforts to strengthen the bond. Investing in the relationship demonstrates your commitment and helps it flourish.

To conclude this chapter I want you to reflect on that fact that elevating your relationships is a key aspect of personal growth and achieving an extraordinary life. By strengthening connections with loved ones, fostering positive relationships, and removing toxic influences, you create a supportive and enriching environment. Remember that relationships are dynamic and require continuous effort and investment. Embrace the journey of nurturing and enhancing your relationships, and let these connections become a source of joy, support, and inspiration on your path to an extraordinary life

CHAPTER 9

Staying Committed to the Climb

Consistency is crucial in any transformation. This chapter provides strategies for staying committed to the journey, even when motivation wanes. I want to emphasize the importance of accountability and shares actionable tips for keeping the faith strong, the body healthy and and your journey on track. Consistency is the bedrock of any successful transformation. Whether you're pursuing personal growth, striving for wellness, or deepening your faith, maintaining commitment to your journey is crucial.

1. Understanding the Role of Consistency

Consistency is more than just a daily habit; it's the steady rhythm that drives long-term success. It involves adhering to routines, maintaining focus, and continually pushing forward, even when progress seems slow. Consistency helps solidify habits, build momentum, and create a sense of stability in your journey.

Understanding that consistency is key helps you frame your approach to transformation. It's about committing to the process, valuing small steps, and recognizing that each effort contributes to your overall progress. Embrace the concept that consistency often yields greater results than occasional bursts of intense effort.

2. Setting Clear and Achievable Goals

Clear, achievable goals serve as a roadmap for your journey and help maintain focus. Here's how to set and refine your goals to stay committed:

Define Specific Objectives:

Make your goals specific and measurable. Instead of a vague goal like "get fit," set a concrete objective such as "exercise for 30 minutes five times a week." Specific goals provide clarity and make it easier to track progress.

Break Goals into Manageable Steps:

Divide larger goals into smaller, manageable tasks. This approach makes the process less overwhelming and allows you to celebrate incremental achievements. For example, if your goal is to improve your faith, start with daily meditation or scripture reading and gradually build from there.

Create a Timeline:
Establish a timeline for achieving your goals. Having deadlines helps create a sense of urgency and keeps you focused. Ensure your timeline is realistic and aligns with your overall objectives.

3. Building a Routine

A consistent routine fosters discipline and helps integrate new habits into your daily life. Here's how to build and maintain an effective routine:

Establish Daily and Weekly Habits:

Incorporate daily and weekly habits that support your goals. For instance, if you're focusing on weight loss, plan your meals and workouts in advance. Consistent habits become second nature and reinforce your commitment.

Create a Structured Schedule:

Develop a structured schedule that includes time for your goals, such as exercise, personal growth activities, or faith practices. A well-organized schedule helps prioritize your commitments and ensures you allocate time for what matters most.

Use Reminders and Tools:

Utilize reminders and tools to stay on track. Set alarms, use calendar apps, or keep a journal to track your progress and remind yourself of your commitments. These tools help reinforce consistency and keep you accountable.

4. Staying Motivated

Motivation can ebb and flow, but maintaining a steady commitment requires strategies to boost and sustain motivation:

Celebrate Small Wins:

Acknowledge and celebrate your achievements, no matter how small. Recognizing progress helps maintain motivation and reinforces your commitment. Keep a record of your accomplishments to remind yourself of how far you've come.

Visualize Success:

Regularly visualize the successful outcome of your goals. Imagine the benefits of achieving your objectives and how it will impact your life. Visualization helps maintain focus and provides a motivational boost during challenging times.

Stay Inspired:

Surround yourself with sources of inspiration. Read motivational books, listen to uplifting podcasts, or connect with like-minded individuals. Inspiration can reignite your passion and keep you engaged in your journey.

5. Maintaining Accountability

Accountability is a powerful tool for staying committed. It involves taking responsibility for your actions and progress, and it can significantly enhance your dedication:

Share Your Goals with Others:

Communicate your goals to trusted friends, family members, or mentors. Sharing your objectives creates a support system and encourages you to stay accountable. Others can provide encouragement, check in on your progress, and offer constructive feedback.

Seek an Accountability Partner:

Find an accountability partner who shares similar goals or interests. Regularly check in with each other, set joint milestones, and support each other's efforts. Having a partner adds a layer of commitment and motivation.

Track Your Progress:

Maintain a journal or use apps to track your progress.

Documenting your journey helps you see how far you've come and identify areas for improvement. Regular tracking keeps you focused and accountable.

6. Navigating Challenges and Setbacks

Challenges and setbacks are inevitable, but how you handle them is crucial for maintaining commitment:

Develop Resilience:

Cultivate resilience by viewing setbacks as learning opportunities rather than failures. Analyze what went wrong, adapt your approach, and use the experience to strengthen your resolve. Resilience helps you bounce back and stay committed despite obstacles.

Adjust Your Plan:

Be flexible and willing to adjust your plan as needed. If you encounter unforeseen challenges, reassess your goals and strategies. Making necessary adjustments ensures that you stay on track and continue moving forward.

Maintain a Positive Mindset:

Stay positive and focused on your long-term vision. A positive mindset helps you persevere through difficulties and keeps you motivated. Practice self-compassion and remind yourself that setbacks are a natural part of the journey.

7. Reinforcing Your Faith and Wellness

Integrating faith and wellness practices into your routine reinforces your commitment to personal growth:

Strengthen Your Faith:

Continue nurturing your faith through regular practices such as prayer, meditation, or scripture reading. Deepening your spiritual connection provides strength and guidance throughout your journey.

Prioritize Wellness:

Maintain a healthy lifestyle by prioritizing physical and mental wellness. Regular exercise, balanced nutrition, and adequate rest contribute to overall well-being and support your commitment to your goals.

Overall, it is important to remember, staying committed to the climb requires consistent effort, motivation, and accountability. By setting clear goals, building a routine, staying motivated, maintaining accountability, and navigating challenges with resilience, you can stay dedicated to your journey. Remember that consistency is the key to long-term success and personal growth. Embrace the process, celebrate your progress, and continue climbing toward your extraordinary life with unwavering commitment and determination.

CHAPTER 10

Reaching the Summit and Beyond

This chapter discusses how to maintain an extraordinary life once you've reached your goals. I offer advice on setting new goals, continuing to grow in faith, and sustaining a healthy lifestyle. Readers will be encouraged to keep climbing, as there is always room for growth and new summits to conquer.

Reaching the summit of your goals is a significant achievement, but it's not the end of the journey—rather, it's a new beginning. This final chapter focuses on how to maintain an extraordinary life once you've achieved your initial goals. Winsome offers guidance on setting new objectives, continuing to grow in faith, and sustaining a healthy lifestyle. You'll be encouraged to embrace ongoing growth and exploration, understanding that there are always new peaks to climb and opportunities to seize.

1. Celebrating Your Achievements
Before moving forward, take time to celebrate your accomplishments. Acknowledging and celebrating your success is crucial for recognizing the effort you've put in and appreciating the progress you've made.

Reflect on Your Journey: Look back on the path you've traveled to reach your summit. Reflect on the challenges you've overcome, the lessons you've learned, and the growth you've experienced. This reflection reinforces the significance of your achievements and builds a sense of fulfillment.

Celebrate with Gratitude: Express gratitude for the support and resources that helped you reach your goals. Whether it's through a personal celebration, sharing your success with loved ones, or giving back to the community, celebrating with gratitude enhances your sense of accomplishment and joy.

Document Your Success: Create a record of your achievements to inspire future endeavors. Write about your journey, take photographs, or compile a list of milestones reached. This documentation serves as a reminder of your capabilities and provides motivation for future goals.

2. Setting New Goals

Achieving your initial goals opens the door to new opportunities and challenges. Setting new goals ensures that you continue to grow and evolve. Here's how to approach setting and pursuing new objectives:

Identify New Aspirations: Reflect on what excites you and what areas you want to explore next. New goals could be related to personal development, career advancements, spiritual growth, or other areas of interest. Choose goals that align with your passions and values.

Build on Past Successes: Use your previous accomplishments as a foundation for new goals. Consider how the skills and experiences gained from reaching your initial goals can be applied to new challenges. Building on past successes helps you leverage your strengths and continue progressing.

Set Stretch Goals: Challenge yourself with goals that push your limits and encourage growth. Stretch goals inspire innovation, creativity, and higher levels of achievement. Ensure that these goals are still realistic and attainable, balancing ambition with practicality.

Create a Plan: Develop a clear plan for achieving your new goals. Outline the steps required, set deadlines, and identify potential obstacles. A structured plan keeps you focused and organized as you embark on your new journey.

3. Continuing to Grow in Faith

Faith is an ongoing journey that requires continuous nurturing and development. Sustaining and deepening your faith is essential for maintaining an extraordinary life:

Engage in Regular Spiritual Practices: Maintain consistent spiritual practices such as prayer, meditation, or attending religious services. Regular engagement with your faith strengthens your connection and provides guidance and support.

Seek New Spiritual Insights: Explore new aspects of your faith and seek opportunities for spiritual growth. This could involve studying religious texts, attending workshops, or participating in faith-based communities. Expanding your understanding of your faith enriches your spiritual journey.

Share Your Faith: Share your spiritual experiences and insights with others. Engaging in discussions about faith, participating in community service, or mentoring others in their spiritual journey fosters a sense of purpose and reinforces your commitment to faith.

4. Sustaining a Healthy Lifestyle
Maintaining a healthy lifestyle is key to sustaining your extraordinary life. Continuing to prioritize physical, mental, and emotional well-being ensures that you remain vibrant and resilient:

Maintain Balanced Nutrition: Continue to make healthy dietary choices that support your well-being. Emphasize a balanced diet with a variety of nutrients, and make mindful eating choices that align with your health goals.

Stay Active: Keep up with regular physical activity to promote overall health and vitality. Find enjoyable forms of exercise that fit your lifestyle, and incorporate movement into your daily routine.

Practice Self-Care: Prioritize self-care practices that support mental and emotional health. This can include relaxation techniques, hobbies, and activities that bring you joy. Regular self-care helps manage stress and enhances your overall quality of life.

Set Wellness Goals: Establish ongoing wellness goals to maintain and improve your health. These goals can focus on areas such as sleep, stress management, or fitness. Setting and pursuing wellness goals helps you stay motivated and committed to a healthy lifestyle.

5. Embracing Continuous Growth

An extraordinary life is characterized by a commitment to continuous growth and exploration. Embrace the idea that reaching one summit is merely a stepping stone to new heights:

Adopt a Growth Mindset: Cultivate a mindset that embraces learning and growth. View challenges as opportunities for development and remain open to new experiences and knowledge. A growth mindset fosters resilience and adaptability.

Explore New Interests: Continuously seek out new interests and passions. Exploring diverse activities and hobbies keeps life exciting and enriches your personal development. Embrace curiosity and remain open to discovering new facets of yourself.

Engage in Lifelong Learning: Commit to lifelong learning by pursuing education, acquiring new skills, and staying informed about developments in your areas of interest. Lifelong learning keeps your mind active and supports ongoing personal and professional growth.

Inspire Others: Share your journey and experiences with others to inspire and motivate them. Your story of reaching the summit and continuing to climb can serve as a powerful example and encourage others to pursue their own extraordinary lives.

6. Finding New Summits to Conquer

The journey of personal growth is a continual ascent, with new summits to conquer and new goals to achieve. Embrace the excitement of the climb and the possibilities that lie ahead:

Set New Challenges: Continuously challenge yourself with new goals and aspirations. Each new challenge provides an opportunity to grow and achieve greater heights. Embrace the journey with enthusiasm and determination.

Celebrate Progress Along the Way: As you pursue new goals, celebrate your progress and milestones. Acknowledge the efforts and achievements along the way, and use them as motivation to keep climbing.

Reflect and Adapt: Periodically reflect on your journey

and adapt your goals as needed. Life's circumstances and priorities may change, and being flexible allows you to stay aligned with your evolving aspirations.

In conclusion, I want to reiterate that reaching the summit is a remarkable achievement, but the journey of personal growth and transformation continues. By celebrating your successes, setting new goals, continuing to grow in faith, and maintaining a healthy lifestyle, you can sustain an extraordinary life. Embrace the process of continuous growth, explore new summits, and remain committed to the climb. Your journey is a testament to your resilience, dedication, and capacity for greatness. Keep climbing, and remember that each summit reached is a stepping stone to new heights and new possibilities.

30-DAY PERSONAL GROWTH, FAITH, AND WEIGHT-LOSS CHALLENGE

Welcome to the 30-Day Personal Growth, Faith, and Weight-Loss Challenge! You have reached or almost reached the summit and now its time to go beyond. However, what happens beyond? I want you to avoid having the feeling of the mountain top experience without a strog foundation to sustain it. This structured 30-day challenge combines faith-based activities, personal growth exercises, and weight-loss strategies into your daily routine. Each day will be structured and the challenge is designed to be repeatable and adaptable to any lifestyle.

Each day includes a scripture or affirmation, a personal growth task, a physical activity challenge, and a nutrition tip or healthy recipe idea. This holistic approach supports your journey to a more extraordinary life by fostering spiritual, mental, and physical well-being.

How to Use This Challenge

Commit to Daily Participation:

Dedicate time each day to complete the daily activities and tasks. Consistency is key to making lasting changes and achieving your goals.

Use the Reflection Space:

Take a few moments each day to reflect on your experiences, progress, and any insights gained. This space helps you stay connected to your journey and track your growth.

Adapt as Needed:

Feel free to adjust the activities to fit your lifestyle and needs. The challenge is meant to be flexible and supportive of your unique journey.

Daily Structure

Each day of the challenge includes the following components:

Daily Scripture or Affirmation:

Begin each day with a scripture or positive affirmation to inspire and ground you. Use this as a source of motivation and reflection.

Personal Growth Task:

Engage in a daily task designed to support your personal development. This might include journaling, setting intentions, or practicing mindfulness.

Physical Activity Challenge:

Incorporate a physical activity to promote weight loss and overall health. Activities range from simple exercises to more vigorous workouts.

Nutrition Tip or Healthy Recipe Idea:

Follow a nutrition tip or try a healthy recipe to support your weight-loss goals and maintain a balanced diet.

Reflection and Progress Tracking:

Use the provided space to document your thoughts, progress, and any challenges encountered. Reflect on how the daily activities impact your growth and well-being.

30-Day Challenge Overview

Week 1: Foundations of Growth

Day 1

Scripture/Affirmation: "I can do all things through Christ who strengthens me." — Philippians 4:13

Personal Growth Task: Set a clear intention for this challenge. Write down your goals and what you hope to achieve.

Physical Activity Challenge: 15-minute brisk walk.

Nutrition Tip/Recipe Idea: Start your day with a nutritious smoothie. Blend spinach, banana, and almond milk.

Reflection: How do you feel about starting this challenge? What are your expectations?

_____
_____
_____
_____

Day 2

Scripture/Affirmation: "The Lord is my shepherd; I shall not want." — Psalm 23:1

Personal Growth Task: Journal about a recent accomplishment and how it made you feel.

Physical Activity Challenge: 20 minutes of gentle stretching or yoga.

Nutrition Tip/Recipe Idea: Prepare a colorful salad with mixed greens, cherry tomatoes, and grilled chicken.

Reflection: What did you learn about yourself through your journaling?

_____
_____
_____
_____

Day 3

Scripture/Affirmation: "Be still, and know that I am God." — Psalm 46:10

Personal Growth Task: Practice a 5-minute meditation focusing on gratitude.

Physical Activity Challenge: 20-minute home workout including squats and lunges.

Nutrition Tip/Recipe Idea: Snack on a handful of almonds and a piece of fruit.

Reflection: How did the meditation influence your mood

today?

_____
_____
_____
_____

Day 4

Scripture/Affirmation: "Trust in the Lord with all your heart and lean not on your own understanding." — Proverbs 3:5

Personal Growth Task: Set a small, achievable goal for the week and plan steps to achieve it.

Physical Activity Challenge: 30-minute walk or jog.

Nutrition Tip/Recipe Idea: Enjoy a healthy dinner of baked salmon with quinoa and steamed vegetables.

Reflection: What is your goal for the week, and how do you plan to reach it?

_____
_____
_____
_____

Day 5

Scripture/Affirmation: "For I know the plans I have for you, declares the Lord." — Jeremiah 29:11

Personal Growth Task: Write about a challenge you faced and how you overcame it.

Physical Activity Challenge: 20 minutes of cardio, such as jumping jacks or dancing.

Nutrition Tip/Recipe Idea: Start your day with oatmeal topped with fresh berries.

Reflection: How did reflecting on your challenges affect your outlook?

_____
_____
_____
_____

Day 6

Scripture/Affirmation: "And we know that in all things God works for the good of those who love him." — Romans 8:28

Personal Growth Task: Identify a limiting belief you have and write down how you can reframe it.
Physical Activity Challenge: 30 minutes of moderate exercise, such as cycling or swimming.

Nutrition Tip/Recipe Idea: Make a healthy stir-fry with tofu and a variety of vegetables.

Reflection: What limiting beliefs did you identify, and how can you change them?

_____
_____
_____
_____

Day 7

Scripture/Affirmation: "Let all that you do be done in love." — 1 Corinthians 16:14

Personal Growth Task: Reflect on your week and write about the progress you've made.

Physical Activity Challenge: 30-minute hike or nature walk.

Nutrition Tip/Recipe Idea: Try a homemade vegetable soup with a side of whole-grain bread.

Reflection: How did reflecting on your week help you understand your progress?

_____
_____
_____
_____

Week 2: Deepening Your Commitment

Day 8

Scripture/Affirmation: "The joy of the Lord is your strength." — Nehemiah 8:10

Personal Growth Task: Write a letter to yourself about why you started this challenge and what you hope to achieve.

Physical Activity Challenge: 20 minutes of high-intensity interval training (HIIT).

Nutrition Tip/Recipe Idea: Enjoy a hearty breakfast of scrambled eggs with spinach and whole-grain toast.

Reflection: How did writing the letter to yourself impact your motivation?

_____
_____
_____
_____

Day 9

Scripture/Affirmation: "Be strong and courageous. Do not be afraid; do not be discouraged." — Joshua 1:9

Personal Growth Task: Set aside time to read a personal

development book or article.

Physical Activity Challenge: 25-minute Pilates or core workout.

Nutrition Tip/Recipe Idea: Prepare a quinoa and black bean salad with avocado.

Reflection: What insights did you gain from your reading today?

_____
_____
_____
_____

Day 10

Scripture/Affirmation: "I will never leave you nor forsake you." — Hebrews 13:5
Personal Growth Task: Identify a positive habit you want to build and create a plan to integrate it into your routine.

Physical Activity Challenge: 30 minutes of yoga focusing on flexibility and relaxation.

Nutrition Tip/Recipe Idea: Have a snack of Greek yogurt with a drizzle of honey and some nuts.

Reflection: How will the new habit benefit your daily life?

_____
_____

_____
_____

Day 11

Scripture/Affirmation: "Let your light shine before others." — Matthew 5:16

Personal Growth Task: Perform a random act of kindness and write about the experience.

Physical Activity Challenge: 30-minute brisk walk or jog.

Nutrition Tip/Recipe Idea: Try a smoothie bowl with mixed fruits and chia seeds.

Reflection: How did performing an act of kindness make you feel?
_____
_____
_____
_____

Day 12

Scripture/Affirmation: "Peace I leave with you; my peace I give you." — John 14:27

Personal Growth Task: Practice a relaxation technique, such as deep breathing or progressive muscle relaxation.

Physical Activity Challenge: 20 minutes of light strength training with bodyweight exercises.

Nutrition Tip/Recipe Idea: Prepare a vegetable stir-fry with tofu and brown rice.

Reflection: How did the relaxation technique impact your stress levels?
_____
_____
_____
_____

Day 13

Scripture/Affirmation: "Cast all your anxiety on him because he cares for you." — 1 Peter 5:7

Personal Growth Task: Write about a recent worry and how you can address it with a positive mindset.

Physical Activity Challenge: 30 minutes of cycling or swimming.

Nutrition Tip/Recipe Idea: Enjoy a salad with roasted chickpeas and a lemon-tahini dressing.

Reflection: How did addressing your worry affect your

outlook?

_____
_____
_____
_____

Day 14

Scripture/Affirmation: "The Lord will fight for you; you need only to be still." — Exodus 14:14

Personal Growth Task: Reflect on your progress so far and identify any areas for improvement.

Physical Activity Challenge: 30-minute hike or nature walk.

Nutrition Tip/Recipe Idea: Make a hearty lentil soup with a side of whole-grain bread.

Reflection: What progress have you made, and what changes will you make going forward?

_____
_____
_____
_____

Week 3: Building Momentum

Day 15

Scripture/Affirmation: "With God all things are possible." — Matthew 19:26

Personal Growth Task: Write about a time you faced a significant challenge and how faith helped you overcome it.

Physical Activity Challenge: 30 minutes of strength training, focusing on major muscle groups.

Nutrition Tip/Recipe Idea: Try a quinoa and roasted vegetable bowl with a light vinaigrette.
Reflection: How did reflecting on your past challenges and faith influence your current mindset?

_____
_____
_____
_____

Day 16

Scripture/Affirmation: "The Lord is my light and my salvation." — Psalm 27:1

Personal Growth Task: Create a vision board or list of long-term goals and aspirations.

Physical Activity Challenge: 30-minute brisk walk or jog.

Nutrition Tip/Recipe Idea: Prepare a smoothie with kale, apple, and flaxseeds.

Reflection: How did creating a vision board or list of goals inspire you for the future?

_____
_____
_____
_____

Day 17

Scripture/Affirmation: "You are the light of the world." — Matthew 5:14

Personal Growth Task: Set aside time for self-reflection and identify areas of your life where you want to make positive changes.

Physical Activity Challenge: 20 minutes of Pilates focusing on core strength.

Nutrition Tip/Recipe Idea: Enjoy a whole-grain wrap with lean turkey, spinach, and avocado.

Reflection: What areas of your life are you focusing on for improvement, and why?

_____
_____
_____
_____

Day 18

Scripture/Affirmation: "I am the vine; you are the branches." — John 15:5

Personal Growth Task: Develop a daily routine that incorporates activities for personal growth, faith, and wellness.

Physical Activity Challenge: 30-minute bike ride or swimming session.

Nutrition Tip/Recipe Idea: Snack on fresh carrot sticks with hummus.

Reflection: How does your new routine support your goals and well-being?
_____
_____
_____
_____

Day 19

Scripture/Affirmation: "God is our refuge and strength, an ever-present help in trouble." — Psalm 46:1

Personal Growth Task: Write about a time when you felt particularly supported by your faith or community.

Physical Activity Challenge: 25 minutes of bodyweight exercises, such as squats and push-ups.

Nutrition Tip/Recipe Idea: Prepare a fresh fruit salad with a drizzle of honey and a sprinkle of nuts.

Reflection: How did reflecting on your support systems enhance your appreciation for them?

_____
_____
_____
_____

Day 20

Scripture/Affirmation: "The peace of God, which transcends all understanding, will guard your hearts and your minds." — Philippians 4:7

Personal Growth Task: Practice mindfulness for 10 minutes and focus on your breathing and present moment awareness.

Physical Activity Challenge: 30 minutes of moderate cardio, such as a dance workout.

Nutrition Tip/Recipe Idea: Enjoy a simple and nutritious meal of grilled chicken with steamed broccoli and sweet potatoes.

Reflection: How did mindfulness affect your mental state today?

_____
_____
_____
_____

Day 21

Scripture/Affirmation: "Trust in the Lord with all your heart." — Proverbs 3:5

Personal Growth Task: Reflect on a recent success and identify the factors that contributed to it.

Physical Activity Challenge: 30-minute hike or nature walk.

Nutrition Tip/Recipe Idea: Make a healthy vegetable stir-fry with tofu and a side of brown rice.

Reflection: What contributed to your recent success, and how can you build on it?
_____
_____
_____
_____

Week 4: Consolidating Your Transformation

Day 22

Scripture/Affirmation: "The Lord is gracious and compassionate." — Psalm 145:8

Personal Growth Task: Write a letter to yourself about how

you've grown throughout the challenge.

Physical Activity Challenge: 30 minutes of strength training with free weights or resistance bands.

Nutrition Tip/Recipe Idea: Try a nutritious breakfast of overnight oats with chia seeds and fresh berries.

Reflection: How did writing a letter to yourself help you appreciate your growth?

_____
_____
_____
_____

Day 23

Scripture/Affirmation: "You are fearfully and wonderfully made." — Psalm 139:14

Personal Growth Task: Identify and write about three personal strengths and how they've helped you during the challenge.

Physical Activity Challenge: 30 minutes of moderate exercise, such as jogging or cycling.

Nutrition Tip/Recipe Idea: Prepare a hearty lentil salad with mixed greens and a light lemon dressing.

Reflection: How do recognizing your strengths affect your confidence and motivation?

_____
_____
_____
_____

Day 24

Scripture/Affirmation: "Let us run with endurance the race that is set before us." — Hebrews 12:1

Personal Growth Task: Create a plan for continuing your personal growth, faith, and wellness journey beyond the challenge.

Physical Activity Challenge: 25 minutes of high-intensity interval training (HIIT).

Nutrition Tip/Recipe Idea: Enjoy a healthy quinoa and black bean stuffed bell pepper.

Reflection: What are your plans for maintaining and expanding on the progress you've made?
_____
_____
_____

Day 25

Scripture/Affirmation: "For God has not given us a spirit of fear, but of power, love, and a sound mind." — 2 Timothy

1:7

Personal Growth Task: Reflect on a fear or limiting belief you've overcome and write about how you did it.

Physical Activity Challenge: 30 minutes of yoga focusing on relaxation and flexibility.

Nutrition Tip/Recipe Idea: Prepare a smoothie with spinach, mango, and almond milk.

Reflection: How did overcoming your fear or belief change your perspective?

_____
_____
_____
_____

Day 26

Scripture/Affirmation: "The Lord is my strength and my shield." — Psalm 28:7

Personal Growth Task: Write about how your faith has been a source of strength during this challenge.

Physical Activity Challenge: 30-minute bike ride or swim.

Nutrition Tip/Recipe Idea: Enjoy a healthy dinner of grilled shrimp with a side of mixed vegetables.

Reflection: In what ways has your faith provided strength

and resilience?

_____
_____
_____
_____

Day 27

Scripture/Affirmation: "Whatever you do, work at it with all your heart." — Colossians 3:23

Personal Growth Task: Set a new personal or professional goal and outline steps to achieve it.

Physical Activity Challenge: 20 minutes of circuit training with a mix of cardio and strength exercises.

Nutrition Tip/Recipe Idea: Try a fresh cucumber and tomato salad with a light vinaigrette.

Reflection: How does setting a new goal help you envision your future?

_____
_____
_____
_____

Day 28

Scripture/Affirmation: "Be joyful in hope, patient in affliction, faithful in prayer." — Romans 12:12

Personal Growth Task: Reflect on how you've maintained hope and patience throughout the challenge.

Physical Activity Challenge: 30 minutes of moderate activity, such as a brisk walk or jog.

Nutrition Tip/Recipe Idea: Enjoy a healthy breakfast of scrambled eggs with spinach and whole-grain toast.

Reflection: How has maintaining hope and patience impacted your journey?
_____
_____
_____
_____

Day 29

Scripture/Affirmation: "I will instruct you and teach you in the way you should go." — Psalm 32:8

Personal Growth Task: Review your progress throughout the challenge and write about the key lessons learned.
Physical Activity Challenge: 30 minutes of your favorite form of exercise.

Nutrition Tip/Recipe Idea: Prepare a nutritious meal of baked chicken with a side of roasted sweet potatoes and green beans.

Reflection: What are the most important lessons you've learned, and how will you apply them going forward?

Day 30

Scripture/Affirmation: "The Lord bless you and keep you." — Numbers 6:24

Personal Growth Task: Celebrate your completion of the challenge and set intentions for continuing your journey of growth.

Physical Activity Challenge: 30-minute relaxation activity, such as a gentle yoga session or a walk in nature.

Nutrition Tip/Recipe Idea: Treat yourself to a wholesome and satisfying meal of your choice, incorporating all the healthy practices you've learned.

Reflection: How do you feel about completing the challenge, and what are your next steps?
_____
_____
_____
_____

The End.

CALL TO ACTION

*Your Journey Continues with
Personal Coaching*

You've reached the end of the challenge but the start of a new beautiful beginning to your extraordinary journey. Take the next step on their journey by signing up for personal coaching sessions with me. There are many benefits to personalized guidance and support. Kindly visit my website, www.winsomecampbell.com, to learn more about the coaching options available and to start transforming your life with one-on-one coaching.

Congratulations on completing the 30-Day Personal Growth, Faith, and Weight-Loss Challenge! Your dedication and commitment to this transformative journey are commendable, and you've already taken significant steps towards a more extraordinary life. But remember, the climb doesn't end here. The next step in your journey towards lasting change and fulfillment is within your reach through personalized coaching with me, Winsome Campbell.

Why Personal Coaching?

Personal coaching offers a unique opportunity for tailored guidance, unwavering support, and accountability as you continue your climb. Here's why engaging in one-on-one coaching can make a profound difference in your life:

Customized Guidance:

Unlike general advice, personal coaching is tailored to your individual needs, goals, and challenges. Together, we will craft a plan that aligns with your unique aspirations, ensuring that every step you take is purposeful and effective.

Accountability and Motivation:

With regular coaching sessions, you'll have a dedicated partner to keep you accountable and motivated. We'll celebrate your successes and navigate through any obstacles, maintaining your focus and commitment to your goals.

Deepened Insights:

Coaching provides a space for deep reflection and self-discovery. Through insightful conversations and targeted exercises, you'll gain a clearer understanding of yourself, your desires, and how to overcome barriers.

Practical Strategies:

Benefit from practical strategies and tools designed to accelerate your growth in personal development, faith, and wellness. We'll work together to implement actionable steps that drive real, measurable results.

Ongoing Support:

Life is a continuous journey, and having a coach means you'll always have support when you need it. Whether you're facing new challenges or striving for new heights, I'll be there to guide and encourage you every step of the way.

Start Your Transformation Today

Are you ready to continue your journey and achieve even greater results? Visit my website at www.winsomecampbell.com to learn more about the coaching options available and to schedule your first session. Whether you're seeking to enhance your personal growth, deepen your faith, or improve your wellness, personalized coaching can provide the support and direction you need to transform your life.

Don't wait any longer—take the next step towards an extraordinary life. Let's climb together, and I'll be honored to support you in reaching new heights.

Visit www.winsomecampbell.com today to begin your coaching journey and unlock your full potential.

ABOUT THE AUTHOR

Winsome Campbell

Winsome Campbell is not just an author; she is a beacon of inspiration dedicated to empowering women to transform their lives from the ordinary to the extraordinary. With an exceptional speaking style honed through her years as a former Toastmaster President, Winsome shares her wealth of knowledge and experiences as both a Life Coach and an educator. With over seven years of classroom teaching experience, she embodies a profound passion for teaching that consistently yields positive results in her students and clients alike.

Since 2010, Winsome has penned over 60 books, each a testament to her commitment to personal development and empowerment. Her journey began in the fast-paced world of corporate banking, where she garnered accolades for being the most outstanding in sales. This background laid the foundation for her belief in the power of networking and connection—key elements she incorporates into her coaching practices to help women navigate their careers with confidence and purpose.

Winsome's dedication to uplifting others extends beyond mere mentorship; it is a reflection of her unwavering love for God, which serves as both her message and motivation. She is on a passionate mission to create a community where women can thrive, embracing their unique strengths and stepping boldly into their destinies.

With Winsome Campbell, audiences discover that the path to an empowered life is accessible, attainable, and filled with promise. Her guidance is a powerful catalyst for transformation, inspiring countless individuals to break barriers and elevate their lives through the art of connection and personal growth.

Made in the USA
Columbia, SC
26 October 2024